D1710344

Written by Stuart A. Kallen

Illustrated by Kristen Copham

Published by Abdo & Daughters, 4940 Viking Drive, Suit 622, Edina, Minnesota 55435.

Library bound edition distributed by Rockbottom Books, Pentagon Tower, P.O. Box 36036, Minneapolis, Minnesota 55435.

Edited by Julie Berg

LIBRARY OF CONGRESS CATALOGING-IN-PUBLICATION DATA

Kallen, Stuart A., 1955-
   If animals could talk / written by Stuart A. Kallen ; [edited by Julie Berg].
        p.   cm. -- (Target Earth)
   Includes bibliographical references.
   Summary: Worms, penguins, elephants, and other animals describe their habitats, physical characteristics, and behavior.
   ISBN 1-56239-187-9
   1. Animals -- Juvenile literature. [1. Animals.] I. Berg, Julie.   II. Title.
III Series.
   QL49.K29   1993
   591.5--dc20   93-18958
   [B]   CIP
                                              AC

Thanks To The Trees Form Which This Recycled Paper Was First Made.

Abdo & Daughters
Minneapolis

They would...

Bark, chatter, twitter and sing. Have a whale of a

time hopping from page to page. Listen to the

animals' stories and learn how you can help save

them.

id you know that animals could talk? Monkeys chatter. Frogs croak. Birds twitter and sing. There are so many different kinds of animals that share the Earth with us. Let's hear what some of our animal friends have to say.

Hello up there! Don't squirm. I'm a worm! I am an important animal. Life would not exist without worms because we help plants grow. Did you know there are more than 7,000 kinds of worms?

My favorite place to live is deep in the soil. The holes I live in are called *burrows*. There are as many as three million of us in one acre (.4 hectares) of land! That's a lot of worms. All those worm holes let the rain water down into the soil. This helps plants grow strong and tall.

I eat all kinds of *organic* matter. Some of my favorite foods are celery, carrot tops, and cabbage. After I'm done eating, I leave a waste product called *castings*. Worm castings are rich in minerals and make great *fertilizer*.

You may think the Earth will never run out of worms. But I have many natural enemies. Moles eat thousands of worms every day. Birds, lizards, frogs, skunks, rats, snakes, and gophers also eat worms. In some parts of the world, even humans eat worms.

The biggest threat to worms are *pesticides.* Farmers spray pesticides on their fields to kill insects that are eating their crops. People put pesticides on their lawns to kill bugs. But those chemicals wash into the soil and kill all the earthworms that live there.

hen the crops don't get our natural fertilizer and need man-made fertilizer. With no worm holes, the rain doesn't wash into the soil properly. Well, it's time for me to slither back into my burrow and let some bigger animals talk to you. But remember, all animals are important, even worms.

What's black and white and black and white and black and white? A penguin tumbling down an iceberg. Ha! I'll bet you didn't know penguins told jokes. Penguins are funny birds.

Even though we're birds, we can't fly. And when we walk around on land, we waddle or hop. When we go down a hill of ice or snow, we ski down on our bellies. Humans think we're funny to watch.

Our bodies are covered with three layers of oily feathers. This keeps us dry and warm in the cold Antarctic climate where we live. Antarctica is also called the South Pole.

Temperatures at the South Pole are 100 degrees below zero. When female penguins lay eggs, male penguins tuck them under their bellies until they hatch. We huddle together to stay warm in the howling wind, until our babies hatch. Female penguins go off for food while male penguins "baby-sit" the eggs.

Some of the other animals that live in the South Pole are walruses, seals, and giant whales. But humans have hunted some of us to near *extinction.*

illions of seals have been killed for their fur. Whales have been killed for food and for their blubber. There are plenty of penguins around, but *water pollution* and oil spills threaten us. Like you, we need clean water to live healthy lives.

Hello down there! I'm an elephant. I'm about the
biggest thing that walks the Earth. That's because I'm 10 feet
(3m) high and I weigh over ten thousand pounds (4,536kg).
That's more than 50 full grown men. I'm an African elephant
and I live in—you guessed it—Africa!

Even though I'm a huge creature, I only eat plants. But I eat a lot of them—over four hundred pounds (181kg) a day. That means I have to eat most of the time. And all that eating makes me thirsty. I drink 18 gallons (68 liters) of water every day.

I use my trunk to pick up food and put it in my mouth. When I drink, I suck water into my trunk and squirt it in my mouth. When two elephants meet, we touch our trunks to each other's–just like people shake hands!

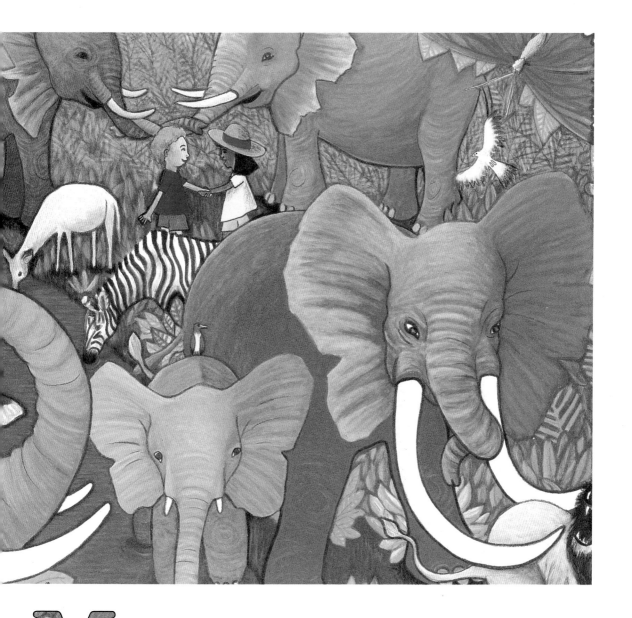

My trunk isn't the only thing sticking out of my face. I have huge ears that I flap back and forth to keep myself cool. And I have two giant teeth ten feet (3m) long. They're called *tusks* and they're made out of ivory. I use my tusks to chase away enemies.

The only animals we fear are humans. Some humans use elephants to work, moving logs and building things. But some humans kill us only for our tusks. They use the ivory to make jewelry and piano keys. This is against the law, but over 100,000 elephants are killed every year just for our ivory tusks.

live in the African grasslands with giraffes, zebras, lions, and cheetahs. Elephants are king of all beasts. But our homes are disappearing as humans build towns and cities onto the grasslands. Soon, there may be no elephants like me left in the wild.

Ahoy, matey! Watch out for that water spray. I'm a whale of a whale, the biggest animal on Earth. How big is big? Just my tongue weighs more than an elephant! How's that for a mouthful! I'm longer than a school bus and weigh more than a semi-truck.

Some people think I'm a fish because I live in the ocean. But I'm no fish. Fish are *cold-blooded*, stay underwater, and breathe through *gills.* I'm a *mammal.* Mammals are *warm-blooded*, like dogs, cats, and even you. I breathe air from a hole in the top of my head. It's called a *blowhole.*

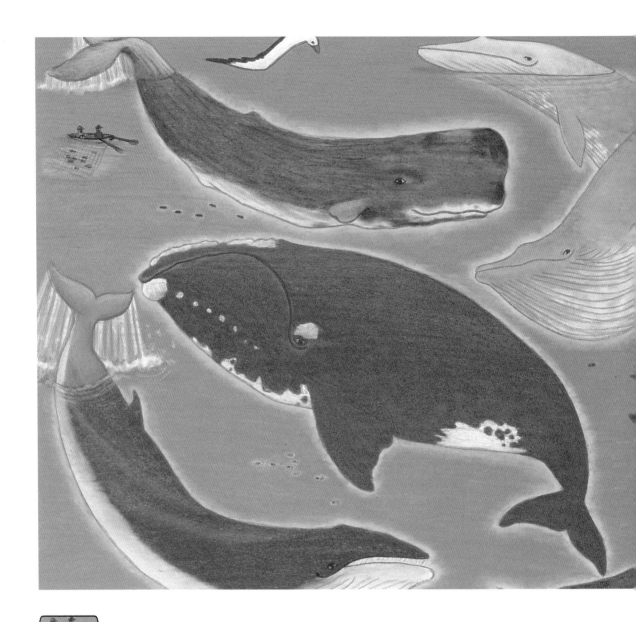

There are over 90 kinds of whales in the world—minke whales, blue whales, right whales, orcas, and sperm whales. I'm a gray whale. In the summer, I live in the cold Arctic waters near the North Pole. In the winter, I swim ten thousand miles (16,090km) down to Mexico. There, female gray whales give birth in the warm waters.

Our bodies are protected by a fatty layer called *blubber*. Blubber keeps us warm in the cold ocean waters. Blubber contains oil. This oil can be burned in lamps. Before electric lights were invented, people all over the world burned whale blubber in their lanterns.

Whales have been hunted for their oil for hundreds of years. Millions of us have been killed. Some countries still hunt whales for food and oil. Someday soon, all whales might be wiped out forever. If so many of us die, we will become *extinct*.

The good news is that people are trying to save the whales. If everyone helps, I'll be sailing the oceans for a long, long time. Well, so long. That's my tale. Now it's time for this whale to sail.

E_{co}—F_{acts}

DANCING FOR DINNER: Wood turtles can't sing for their supper. But they dance for their dinner. The turtle stamps its feet hard on the ground. This shaking makes earthworms rise to the surface. Then the turtle eats them for dinner. No one knows why the worms come out of their holes when the turtle stomps. Maybe the earthworms think when the ground starts shaking, it is raindrops falling. They leave their holes because they think it is raining and don't want to drown underground.

ONE WAY TO WING IT: Penguins' wings look like useless little stubs. They are useless—for flying. But penguins' wings are made for swimming. Penguins can swim 20 miles (32km) an hour. They stay in the water for five months at a time. There they feed on fish, bobbing up for air every few minutes.

EATING LIKE AN ELEPHANT: Elephants' trunks have 40,000 different muscles in them. The trunk is so strong that it can pick up a tree—but it is so sensitive that it can pick a single blade of grass. Elephants can use their huge tusks to dig yams out of the ground. They eat 400 pounds (181kg) of food a day. They have six sets of teeth, one below the other. When one set wears down, another takes its place. When the last tooth is gone, the old elephant can no longer eat and dies.

Glossary

Acre—an area of land about 208 (63m) feet long by 208 feet (63m) wide, or 43,264 square feet (3,969 sq.m.). There are 640 acres (260 hectares) in a square mile.

Blowhole—the hole on top of a whale's head used for breathing. Some whales have two blowholes.

Blubber—the layer of fat that protects animals. Seals, whales and walruses have blubber.

Burrows—holes in the ground that animals live in.

Castings—worm manure.

Cold-blooded—type of animal whose blood temperature changes with air temperature. Fish, insects, and reptiles are cold-blooded.

Extinct—not existing now. Animal species that have all died out are extinct. Dinosaurs are extinct.

Fertilizer—any substance used to enrich the soil so that plants may grow.

Gills—breathing organs for fish. Gills let fish separate oxygen from water. This allows them to "breathe" underwater.

Mammal—a warm-blooded group of animals with hair and a backbone. Humans, dogs, cats, mice, bats, apes, and whales are mammals.

Organic—any substance coming from a living thing. Leaves are organic. Organic fertilizer is made from natural substances, not chemicals.

Pesticide—any substance used to kill insects. Some chemical pesticides harm the enviroment.

Ton—2,000 pounds (907kg).

Tusk—a long pointed tooth that sticks out of the mouth.

Warm-blooded—type of animal whose body temperature stays the same, whatever the outside temperature. Birds and mammals, including humans, are warm-blooded.

Water pollution—dirt and poisons in the water.

TARGET EARTH™ COMMITMENT

At Target, we're committed to the environment. We show this commitment not only through our own internal efforts but also through the programs we sponsor in the communities where we do business.

Our commitment to children and the environment began when we became the Founding International Sponsor for Kids for Saving Earth, a non-profit environmental organization for kids. We helped launch the program in 1989 and supported its growth to three-quarters of a million club members in just three years.

Our commitment to children's environmental education led to the development of an environmental curriculum called Target Earth™, aimed at getting kids involved in their education and in their world.

In addition, we worked with Abdo & Daughters Publishing to develop the Target Earth™ Earthmobile, an environmental science library on wheels that can be used in libraries, or rolled from classroom to classroom.

Target believes that the children are our future and the future of our planet. Through education, they will save the world!

Minneapolis-based Target Stores is an upscale discount department store chain of 517 stores in 33 states coast-to-coast, and is the largest division of Dayton Hudson Corporation, one of the nation's leading retailers.

591.5
Kal

Kallen, Stuart A.

If animals could
talk

DATE DUE	BORROWER	
	Veronical	13 6
	Gloria	11 4
	ArKayll	25

591.5   Kallen, Stuart A.
Kal
          If animals could
          talk

LOCKHART ELEMENTARY SCHOOL

 GUMDROP BOOKS - Bethany, Missouri